#shelfie

#shelfie

how to style and display
your collections

GERALDINE JAMES

CICO BOOKS
LONDON NEW YORK

Published in 2020 by CICO Books
An imprint of Ryland Peters & Small Ltd

20–21 Jockey's Fields
London WC1R 4BW

341 E 116th St
New York, NY 10029

www.rylandpeters.com

10 9 8 7 6 5 4 3 2

Text © Geraldine James 2020
Design and photography © CICO Books
and Ryland Peters and Small 2020

A CIP catalog record for this book is available from the
Library of Congress and the British Library.

ISBN: 978-1-78249-844-5

Printed in China

Editor: Helen Ridge
Designer: Toni Kay
Photographer: for all photography credits, see page 188

In-house editor: Anna Galkina
Art director: Sally Powell
Head of production: Patricia Harrington
Publishing manager: Penny Craig
Publisher: Cindy Richards

Contents

Introduction

I was lucky enough when writing this book to choose from hundreds of beautiful images and put together stories to help readers think about what a shelf can do for them. From bright bursts of color to simple, soothing white collections, there is something here for everyone, whatever their decor or taste.

When considering a new space or home, I always think of the many #shelfie displays that I could create, what they might look like, and all the precious items that will be allocated to each one. For me, it's not only about storage, but how each #shelfie can work as a style statement. They don't replace art in a home, but are considered as living pieces of art in themselves, as a way of dressing an empty wall.

I hope that the themes I have created, from #raw to #shelvesofcuriosities, from #recycled to #pureandsimple trigger your imagination. If you are unsure about the look you would like to create, below are some principles I tend to adhere to as a starting point for shelf inspiration. However, as I always say: rules are meant to be broken, so have fun, experiment, and remember that the best thing about #shelfies is how easily they can be changed.

MY PRINCIPLES OF SHELF DISPLAYS

Tell a story
It is always wise to have a theme or a story in mind, be it nature, collectables, or nostalgic memorabilia.

Varying heights
Make sure you have a selection of objects of various heights, otherwise your display will simply look far too uniform.

Mixed media
Mix up textures such as wood with glass or paper with handmade pottery. This approach always draws the eye as it looks so tactile. If you want to put up shelves, consider using recycled or reclaimed wood, which give lovely texture and individuality.

Use the wall
I like to hang a photograph or painting behind the shelf to give extra height and a backdrop to a display.

Stay off-center
This is a very important principle: start with your largest item and place it off-center, arranging the other objects around it. Trust me, this works!

Layers, layers, layers
Start with the largest objects at the back and the smallest at the front, and slightly vary how you position things as you work along the shelf. Keep experimenting until your display looks balanced.

Curate a gallery of images
Create your very own gallery by displaying art or photographs in abundance on slender shelves with a ridge that helps to support them.

Get creative with color
Color can be added successfully to your home without taking the plunge and painting a wall. I've been collecting green objects for displaying in my otherwise monochrome kitchen and they really add interest.

Play with proportions
Scale is something I feel strongly about and I am not afraid to put large or oversized shelves or units into a small space. It actually does the opposite of what you might expect, opening up the space and giving generous proportions.

Above all, have fun and enjoy your #shelfie journey.

#color

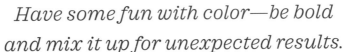

*Have some fun with color—be bold
and mix it up for unexpected results.*

Add a pop of color
to liven up any space

If you simply aren't brave enough to use bold colors in your room decoration, adding them to shelves is a good way of making an eye-catching statement. In this chapter you will see various ways of achieving this. I especially love to paint shelves the same color as the wall behind, to introduce a new dimension to the statement wall.

The mid-century wall unit shown opposite offers a safe space for storing and displaying favorite treasures. Such units, which were very popular at the time, offer complete flexibility—the position of the shelves can be changed quickly and easily for a different look and feel.

Changing the look of a shelf unit by adding wallpaper to the back of the shelves takes less time than painting them. Here, the backdrop of vintage floral wallpaper brings a clever new dimension to the display and balances well with the collection of vintage china and glass. A pile of folded vintage textiles and a glass raised on a stack of dinner plates in similar blues add height, while the rows of vases in matching green create depth. The varying heights and complementary colors bring synergy.

PAGE 10 Although diverse, this collection of objects on a mid-century wall unit works well together. There is an African feel to the display, with a ceramic zebra, two gilt elephants, and a carving of a giraffe alongside, providing a glimpse into a world that the owners love. Boldly colored glassware, art, and books bring added interest.

PAGE 11 This is a perfect example of how to group a small number of decorative objects, starting with the vibrant Pols Potten floral vase, positioned to the side. The flower stems in the blue-and-white vase introduce texture, while the classically shaped table lamp, which mirrors the shape of the fish vase, adds depth as well as lighting the display. The overall effect is stunning.

LEFT Cleverly coordinated glass and china, eclectic but harmonious, and a pile of pink tumblers complement the bright blue vase and pink peony. The floral print echoes the colors and motifs of the wallpaper. The letters "W" and "F" add a personal touch.

OPPOSITE An imaginative and harmonious display of mostly pastel shades makes a big color statement on these kitchen shelves and worktop.

OPPOSITE A collection of colored glass bottles catches the light as it streams through this window framed by trailing grape vines. Originally used for beer or sodas, the bottles make a beautiful and inexpensive decorative display. A bunch of garden roses adds texture to the overall effect.

ABOVE Three similar vintage vases in pale green—two Dartmouth pottery and one milk glass—and a seascape in complementary shades make a gorgeously understated shelf display in an all-white setting.

RIGHT How clever to use hollowed-out red cabbages as vases for a seasonal show of pansies and primulas. They make the perfect addition to a garden room, with garden pencils in a pot and a book introducing height.

A dark paint color on walls makes a space feel luxurious and adds a sense of intrigue. When shelves are painted the same shade, they disappear into the background and the objects displayed on them appear almost as if they are hanging in midair. I love the use of eggplant on the walls and the tub in the bathroom, below, and on the kitchen walls, right. It looks fresh and modern, especially against the white ceilings.

ABOVE The eggplant-painted tongue-and-groove wood paneling on the walls draws attention to the simplest of displays above the fireplace. The wall clock positioned higher than the single shelf and just off to the left makes a quirky statement.

In this sleek and modern kitchen, the long and functional stainless-steel shelf stands out against the eggplant-painted walls. The containers on the shelf and the cooking utensils hanging from it are displayed in an orderly and easy-to-access way, facilitating the preparation of meals and the cleaning of the space.

OPPOSITE TOP LEFT This sunny display features a large and shapely Pols Potten vase, a smaller vase in the same bold yellow, and tiny, yellow ceramic animal ornaments, all grouped together on a shiny yellow credenza.

OPPOSITE TOP RIGHT A strong statement is made with vintage ceramics from the sixties and seventies, the pops of scarlet picked up in the red book and flowers.

OPPOSITE BOTTOM LEFT On top of a blue cabinet, several items overlap one another in an appealing way. The largest item, the canvas, has been cleverly placed off-center, with smaller items layered in front for depth.

OPPOSITE BOTTOM RIGHT United by color and theme, this display on pink-painted shelves features various pieces from tea sets, all decorated with pink roses, to pull the whole scheme together. A collection of interesting teapots on top of the shelves completes this vintage tea story.

ABOVE Perfectly balanced turquoise and orange-red, with carefully selected books and a turquoise pleated lampshade with an orange base, this display has clearly been created with a lot of thought.

A well-thought-out story is being told on the shelves of the turquoise cabinet shown above, with all the basic rules of shelf display in evidence. The table lamp, with its turquoise shade, pulls the story together, while the off-center stack of books in diminishing sizes and the simple chunky pottery pitcher of tulips on top add height. The vibrant orange of the flowers complements the covers of the orange-, red-, and yellow-sleeved books on the upper shelf.

Although color principles are being adhered to here, it is a brave use of color, based on establishing the solid turquoise of the dresser and the lamp first. From there, you can experiment with everything else.

The dark turquoise, custom-made shelf unit in this bedroom features an impressive selection of books. My rules for displaying books are exactly as you see here: some are stacked, some leaning, some straight upright, to keep things interesting. A few decorative objects break the lines, while family photos add a more personal touch.

I love the uniformity of these vintage terracotta
pots of pink and yellow primulas, on display
in an auricula theater. The striking blue paint
on the back of the old glass-fronted cabinet
highlights the pots beautifully.

OPPOSITE This image is so pleasing and illustrates clearly what can be achieved with a tight grouping of unique vessels and objects. Sitting on a dark mantel against a dark-colored wall is a mismatch of unusual vintage items in an assortment of colors.

ABOVE LEFT Each cubbyhole in this blue custom-made shelving unit contains something a little out of the ordinary. I like how the smaller items add scale and perspective to the pictures, which almost fill their space, but without detracting from them.

ABOVE RIGHT Turquoise shelves house everyday china and glass, making it a less-than-ordinary cupboard, accessible but eclectic, a pleasing mix of colors, shapes, and heights.

I find it inspiring to see how much displays can reveal about how a person's mind works. The displays featured here do exactly that, reflecting the unique sense of style and taste of their owners.

Sometimes the architectural shape of an unusual plant or a brave, bold mix of colors produces something quite unexpected and unusual, which is clearly illustrated here. But such displays also show how having a strong color for the background helps to encourage more experimental display choices.

PREVIOUS PAGES How utterly pleasing is this shelf display of well-selected shiny vessels in pastel shades. Relating a clear story, they are arranged according to the principles of off-center; depth, with small in front of big; and texture, from the flowers and foliage. All this with a backdrop of a wonderful swirly complementary wallpaper.

LEFT A high-impact display mostly of a stunning collection of glass from 1950 to 1970. There are varying heights and surface textures, with an emphasis on strong coordinating color. Using a shelf display is the perfect way for this passionate collector to show and display her irreplaceable collection of retro glass. She has made sure to use secure shelf brackets to avoid any accidents.

OPPOSITE In this impressive custom-made shelf unit, the different-sized shelves make it easy to create a unique and eye-catching arrangement using objects of various shapes and sizes. It is a quirky collection that tells you much about the home owner and their interests, and shows the impact that collecting items over time can make. A cool gray paint for the shelves is a great way to create a uniform look.

OPPOSITE Shelves fixed across windows are a really inspired idea, especially when used for collections of colored glass. Against a backdrop of garden foliage, this well-proportioned and well-set-out visual effect shows the light filtering beautifully through the glass. Adding height to the spaces between the shelves are some well-proportioned branches and a row of iridescent cups hanging from hooks.

ABOVE Imagine being the lucky child of such creative parents. A large, shiny yellow armoire has glazed doors to show off all the colorful clothes inside, while a boldly painted plate rack is used as a shelf to display and store toys, books, and more clothes.

These photographs speak volumes about how brave you can be with color, but also how you can use shelves in different ways. I have never put glass shelves in front of my windows, but I am definitely going to give them a try. However, I can't help thinking about the practical side of doing so. The shelves will need lots of cleaning, because the sun will be unkind about showing marks, and there is always the issue of dust collecting on decorative items that don't get used every day.

Collecting things is something that we humans are passionate about. It's to do with the hunt, the challenge of discovering a treasure somewhere new or while on vacation—it makes a strong story and the items that you can find are so collectible.

A chunky floating shelf in a child's bedroom features an interesting and unusual mixture of playthings. Displayed in a single row, they are linked by their strong colors and geometric shapes.

Family and friends will sometimes buy beautiful handmade, design-led toys for children, but these are quite often not what the child wants to play with. As the toys can be valuable, high shelves in a child's bedroom are good places to display them, perhaps until the child is old enough to appreciate them. In the meantime they make a style statement and can be appreciated from afar.

Set alongside a workspace, this tall blue unit of cubbyhole shelves shows how layering different pieces adds depth to a display. Starting with the vintage picture on top, positioned off-center, the rest of the display keeps to the color story, but the addition of strong primary colors keeps it interesting and playful.

The bold use of color by brave home owners was exactly what I had in mind for the pictures in this chapter. Painting floating shelves a strong color is a good place to start if you want to transform your #shelfies. If you're unsure about which color to go for, take a look at the items you want to display and decide on the color that unifies them. Alternatively, you could paint the shelves whatever color appeals to you the most and then choose objects that would make the most winning combination.

LEFT This vintage shelf unit housing everyday kitchen items is functional, but what sets it apart is the vivid pink paintwork, which creates an exciting retro feel. I can only think how underwhelming this display would appear on white shelves with a white background. The lesson to be learned is to push the boundaries.

OPPOSITE This #shelfie, which shows astonishing confidence, is almost more about the deep floating shelves than the objects placed on them. Painted a hypnotic red to match the wallpaper, they host an eclectic display of front-facing books and a mix of treasured objects.

RIGHT The golden touches, from the brackets and door handle to the pots and objects on the shelves, pull this display together, which is offset by the hot pink backdrop and door. The largest items, the plants, are positioned off-center for the greatest impact.

#artandphotography

I like this simple shelf, hung high above the desk. Two monochrome art pieces are propped up against the wall to the right, one overlapping the other, to give depth to the display. A third piece is overlapped by one of the wire baskets, while a hurricane lamp sits slightly off-center. A garland of wood in the same tones links the different elements together.

OPPOSITE What a pleasing #shelfie this is—all white frames (apart from one that's black) of sepia and black-and-white prints. Monochrome, which is very easy to work with, is the theme of the display. All the images sit on narrow picture frame shelves, with a lip to stop them slipping off. In keeping with the color theme, all-white vintage vases in the foreground add depth and context.

*Mixing art and photographs looks great and using old
and new frames makes for a more interesting collection.*

Flexible and inspiring
ideas for your pictures

This chapter addresses the all-important issue of what to do with all your
pictures—paintings and photographs—that you want to have on display.
There are some really inspiring ideas here.

I like to include unusual art or photographs, which I've collected from all
over the world, in among my favorite pictures of family, otherwise the display
may end up looking something like a rogues' gallery. Good-looking frames
are easy to come by these days, but for my most precious pieces of art,
I still prefer to use a professional framer, to help preserve and keep them
in pristine condition.

Pictures don't have to be hung from walls. They can be leaned against them on the floor, propped up on shelves or sideboards—there is so much flexibility that it's easy to change your displays whenever the mood takes you.

A really long shelf in a sitting room or kitchen provides lots of scope for creating a theme, as well as giving the greatest impact to the objects on display. It can also pull a room together, either through color or theme. Creating a display is generally the last thing to do in the decoration of a room, but it is by far the most enjoyable. Remember that scale is important, and mix sizes and shapes on a shelf to add interest and make a bold statement.

ABOVE Anglepoise lamps clamped to this narrow shelf above the kitchen countertop is a good lighting solution. The shelf makes a flexible display space that you can quickly change as and when you like. Postcards and little reminders of events enjoyed, propped up against the wall, are the simplest of things, but they are part of what makes your house your home.

I love everything about this scene. A chest of drawers in dark wood, showing signs of its age, acts as the plinth for a very impressive double portrait in monochrome, almost as wide as the chest. The chest is also large enough to house an iconic table lamp and an assortment of harmonious and interesting objects.

A very long rosewood sideboard acts as a display shelf in this very impressive home. Layers of carefully curated pieces of art and ceramics in cream and parchment, with the largest at the back, provide depth and interest. The organic shapes offset the hard edges of the framed art. Overlapping the pieces piques the curiosity still further.

OPPOSITE This well-balanced display incorporates various colors and textures, but remains true to its central theme of simplicity with a twist. A narrow wood shelf forms the base for some abstract art in a decorative frame, flanked on one side by a pair of candlesticks of different heights. On the other side, a pair of photographs provides visual balance. Modern wooden birds swoop down from the ceiling, adding a quirky touch and tying the colors of the room together.

ABOVE The overall feel of this display is very retro. A vintage school chest is its base, with the focus an art school portrait positioned off-center for extra impact. The black-framed art lines up pleasingly alongside. Two books underneath the small cup give it the height it needs.

RIGHT Warm-colored woods make this selection of art, bowls, and the carved duck appear very considered. The matching narrow lamps with tiny shades add balance.

ABOVE This is a really good example of a busy but well-ordered shelf. By carefully overlapping favorite family photos, it is possible to have more of them on display. A quirky toy placed in the middle introduces variety and a humorous touch.

ABOVE RIGHT The vivid green landscape painting gives a real pop to this otherwise neutral color scheme and brings it to life. Hanging it on the wall above a leaning display creates a sense of height and additional impact.

These two pages show how you can still achieve a sense of order even when using quite a number of items on your shelves. The displays all look balanced and neat, but they have been achieved with a degree of skill, using what I call my principles of shelf display (see page XX), which will help you get started with confidence. After all, it's almost impossible to edit a favorite display, especially of family pictures. Alternatively, you can always change your displays on a regular basis, placing objects in the cupboard until you wish to see them again.

Almost all the shelfies shown here feature a bigger central or off-center piece, with the display being built up by adding height and layering. When satisfied that the leaning wall pictures have been placed to your satisfaction, you can start introducing other objects. Adding organic or round shapes to a shelf of picture frames helps to soften the hard edges.

Bear in mind that busy shelf displays need regular cleaning and dusting, otherwise they can soon start to resemble an old junk shop.

ABOVE LEFT Positioned off-center on a classic-style shelf, a very beautiful, dark portrait photograph, framed in black, is balanced by some dark wooden printers' blocks.

ABOVE RIGHT On the very narrow shelf, simple framed and unframed pictures overlap, inviting scrutiny. Below, on the busy desk, a leaning picture and a pencil holder overlap the black-and-white image hanging off-center on the wall, bringing a certain symmetry to the display.

PAGES 48–49 Dominating this living room, sturdy walnut shelves and their displays sit against a gray concrete wall that is almost industrial in feel. The owner, who has a great eye and a love of the unusual, has chosen an eclectic selection of objects, but they all speak with the same voice.

The neutral tones of the elements at play on these pages—wood, concrete, marble—are all so appealing. Dark walls and dark shelves are all lightened with reflective objects, mixed materials, and different textures, to add interest and soften the overall effect. Scale is used to add drama.

New kitchens generally include display shelves, either for holding everyday china or as an intrinsic part of the overall design. They are then an invitation to add favorite pieces of glassware, even art, and fulfill a need to show off your carefully curated items.

ABOVE This close-up view of the image shown on page 44 illustrates how one color in the piece of art has been selected, in this case black, and items in that color, such as the candlesticks, have been introduced, adding a sense of unity to the display.

LEFT Matching marble has not only been used for the splashback and worktop in this custom-built kitchen, but also for the display shelf above, illustrating how shelves have increasingly become an intrinsic part of kitchen design.

OPPOSITE Simple walnut shelves allow the owner to show off a carefully curated but diverse group of beautiful objects, both modern and mid-century.

In this traditional English cottage, complete with flagstone floor and painted brick walls, a high shelf has been added the length of the zinc-topped sideboard, with a selection of kitchen items and art adding interest to the simplicity.

Prominent dark-wood shelves with dark-metal supports create a distinctly industrial feel. The display, which contains some deeply personal items, including a child's pair of shoes, a vintage camera, and black-and-white photographs in dark-wood frames, keeps the vibe the same.

ABOVE LEFT There is an almost Hollywood vibe to this art deco-style room, with its chrome-framed vintage chairs. Very smart, well-framed iconic black-and-white photographs lean against the wall in an orderly fashion on a specially designed shelf. The photos below are also leaning, but some of them are stacked against each other, inviting inspection.

ABOVE RIGHT AND OPPOSITE The low solid headboard acts as a shelf for a restrained display in the first bedroom. In the second, an exciting mix of multilayered black-and-white photographs and old oil portraits are tightly displayed like a gallery on plain white shelves. Shades of dark brown and black and white together make an appealing palette.

Strong monochrome themes have always been popular and they never fail to impress. Well-framed iconic black-and-white or sepia photographs make for a professional gallery feel and can work well with your own photographs. Shelves built expressly to house them—they should be narrow with a lip to stop the images from tumbling off—can fit into traditional and modern environments alike, and the displays can be quite uniform to achieve the best overall effect. But good framing is essential—there's nothing worse than art or photographs that have slipped in their frames.

Recessed bedside tables have been built into this striking headboard, allowing for two distinct and intimate displays. The headboard also acts as a shelf for two mismatching lamps and three framed figurative pictures. It would have been easy to place these centrally, but see how effective they look positioned off-center.

BELOW Mantels make perfect places for curating a display. On this white marble mantel, the big, bold piece of graffiti art, which sits off-center, pulls the whole display together. Candlesticks add uniformity and height, while the ampersand injects a sense of fun. Layering brings depth and extra interest.

RIGHT Large, empty wooden frames, with photographs pushed into them at different levels, sit on a white, low-level cupboard. In front, a stack of books adds height and color, while some intriguing objects, carefully selected for their design content, help support the purposeful display. The artist's mannequin provides animation, its color echoing that of the frames.

The various pieces of art and photography that we collect need to be edited down from time to time to something that we can be proud to present at home. Selecting your favorite Instagram images, or other people's, is the start of bringing your digital life to real life—it's something I do all the time. Preparing to sit images on a shelf can be simple, but I always ask myself what I want to achieve and what is my theme. Black-and-white images are the most popular choice for photographs, but color ones can also work well, especially if you choose a single common thread, such as the beach or the sea, or grass or woodland, so that the overall effect is one color. Choosing animals and buildings also allows a certain consistency.

In this light and airy office environment, narrow picture shelves hold the various framed artworks in place. I like the mix of sizes and the slightly off-center positioning. Without doubt, this is a very considered display but one that can easily be added to or changed, as with any leaning art or photographic display.

These beautiful stainless steel shelves provide a real contrast to the raw walls and the gleaming wooden vessels placed on them. Vintage wooden finds have been added to the mix, creating a coherent and special display.

OPPOSITE Bursts of bright yellow create a strong connection here. All the vintage items, worn with time, sit on a beaten and gnarled wooden stool, creating a surprising #shelfie with lots of texture.

Objects worn with time are the base for raw shelf displays—they have a way of telling unique stories.

The most natural elements become art

In a raw display, the objects or artifacts on the shelf, and the shelf itself, are in their natural state, and not processed or purified in any way. It's a characteristic that has both charm and individuality. Objects from nature, such as shells and feathers, come into this category, as does artisan pottery. The provenance of an object comes high on the list when making choices for #shelfies. If you are putting items on show, then it's especially important that they come with a story. This adds to their overall charm and can also inspire others. Acquiring such things often comes when you least expect it, so always keep your eye out, especially when walking in the countryside or on a beach.

The mantel of a wooden fire surround, with its original paintwork, is used as a shelf for a diverse and quirky collection of objects that suit their setting perfectly. Even an old bristle brush merits inclusion.

Whether you are beachcombing for shells or driftwood, or searching for interestingly shaped twigs and branches, these raw elements from nature make perfect display items on a shelf. Not only do they come with a story, but they can also accessorize pottery and other craft items so well, adding shape and texture.

Start with a shelf that is made of something untreated or natural, such as stone or wood. Ideally, the wall behind should also be natural, such as limewashed or concrete. A long misshapen twig placed off-center in a glass vase can be the beginnings of your raw shelf display, or a collage of framed pressed flowers, or a row of pebbles—the list is endless, and just think how inexpensive it will be.

ABOVE LEFT Vintage labels of pressed flowers create a charming display on this wall. Such a backdrop would lend itself to the back of a shelf or behind a sideboard, with a display of equally natural or vintage elements in front.

ABOVE Collecting pottery in all shapes and sizes using different firing and glazing techniques can be so absorbing. Traveling opens the door to a wealth of artistic talent, and this shelf shows what beautiful displays can be achieved with pots that have raw texture and color at their heart.

A very long and chunky concrete shelf set low down is attractive as well as functional, with everything on it easily accessible. This is a well-chosen selection of interesting finds, using a variety of raw materials, from a pottery pitcher of branches to earthenware bowls and glass bottles. The entire room reflects this natural theme.

Old and weathered items that tell a story, or items that have had a previous use, are to me what a good raw shelf display is all about. Their story prompts conversation. Trawling through flea markets and vintage stores has always been a real hobby of mine, and I know how important it is not to rush the process—it is the slow and thoughtful acquisition of objects that is always the most interesting. Collecting pieces from different towns or even different countries will change the character of the displays you create. Always consider the material of the shelf you are intending to use for a raw display. Unpolished metal or concrete always look good.

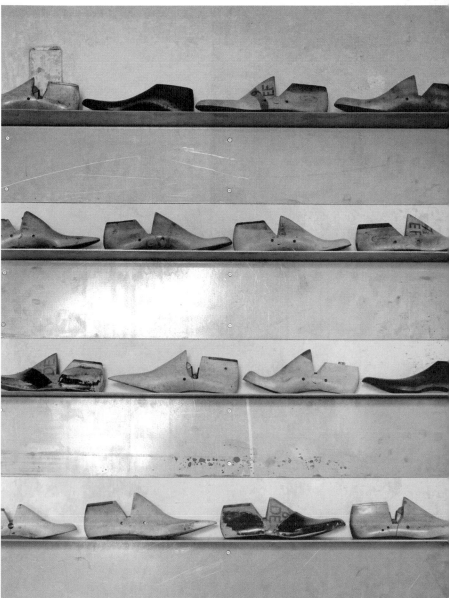

LEFT This perfect composition of vintage wooden chopping boards, displayed with a rusty wire frame inserted between them, and a bottle of olive oil and a rustic stone bowl, offers a pleasing mix of textures and materials.

ABOVE Long metal shelves complement the vintage shoe lasts. I love the humor of this display, with the shoes of different shapes and sizes appearing to march in two different directions. Wooden shoe lasts are easy to come by at flea markets and vintage fairs.

Finding the right shelves when you want to make something quite unique is a matter of thinking outside the box. Objects that had a previous use or life, such as a cart or a piece of old wood that was once a part of something else, create shelves that become an equally interesting and intrinsic part of a display. Never discard anything until you have thought carefully about what you might be able to use it for.

There are always old school, factory, or store fittings to be found at flea markets, and they can inspire you to create something really different.

ABOVE A simple metal shelving unit above an old rustic table enhances the beautifully turned wooden bowls. These have been carefully placed for maximum impact, mixed in with a wooden drafting compass, folding rulers, and other smaller turned pieces. The overall effect is one of great balance.

RIGHT This old shoe rack on wheels has been turned into a ready-made shelf unit. Used to hold Brown Betty teapots and vintage printers' block and metal store-front letters, it is the perfect tea cart.

OPPOSITE Shelves made from old planks of wood offer the perfect structure for an all-wood display. The different-sized spaces between the shelves add interest to the overall feature, as do the small crates and boxes that have been used to introduce height as well as holding objects. The cog-like object right of-center adds dimension and the little items at the bottom add scale.

PREVIOUS PAGES Beneath the original exposed beams of the kitchen in this ancient house runs a magnificent long shelf that the owner uses to store and display everyday objects, such as modern china and glassware. I like the juxtaposition of really old and contemporary, not to mention the splashes of apropos canary yellow.

LEFT A very clever joiner has been at work here to create this eccentric and imaginative wall with the simplest of materials for a child's room. Favorite soft toys have been tucked into the protruding shelves, some of which are deeper than others for variety.

OPPOSITE Reused wood in various finishes makes the most attractive #shelfie for a pleasing and well-curated display of objects that all show signs of wear and tear and evidence of former lives. Shape and materials have all been taken into consideration. The off-center plank of wood is the main focus and the starting point for the placement of everything else.

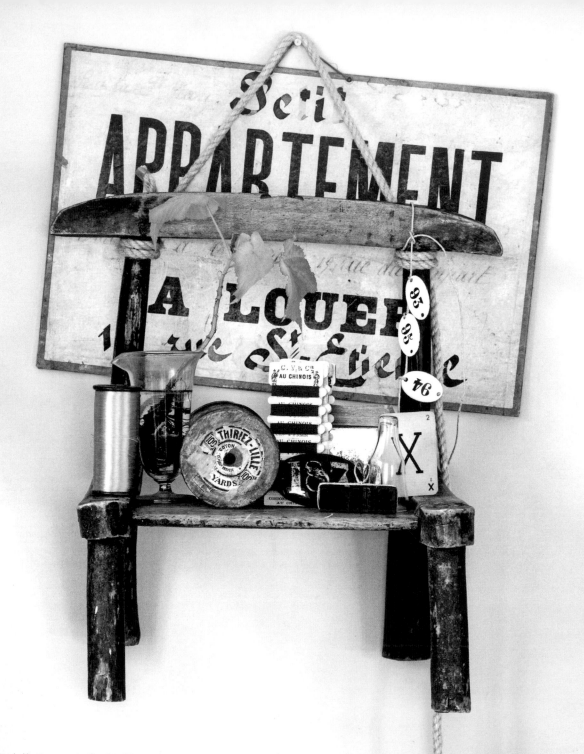

OPPOSITE What an original idea to use a tiny vintage chair as a shelf. Everything displayed on it looks as though it comes from a sewing box of a similar age, providing a linking theme. The old French "Apartment to rent" sign acts as a backdrop and helps to fill the white wall void of this very inspiring display.

ABOVE Sometimes all that's needed to house a display is a very simple white shelf. Pulling this scheme together is a creamy yellow color, as seen in the postcard of an Egon Schiele painting, which sits so well behind the two wooden apples.

Being disciplined with color and having a fine eye for detail when picking items or finishes will ensure that all the objects you choose really sit well together, so that you can create the perfect display, no matter how simple. A good imagination also helps. Recognizing on your travels which rare finds will work and which won't, no matter how much you love them, is another important discipline. You never know where you will find the perfect addition to the next shelf display, so make the most of every opportunity and head straight to your nearest flea market or thrift shop.

OPPOSITE Fitting in perfectly in this rustic kitchen, these ingenious shelves are made from old church pew seats held up with thin metal brackets. The display of both old and new everyday kitchen implements, big pottery pitchers, mugs, and baskets, is not only practical but also very pleasing in its layout and limited color palette.

THIS PAGE I love everything about this display. A small lip on the high shelf provides support for the vintage letters and objects that spell out the owner's name. Texture and color are provided by the raw wall above the smooth plastered wall. The angled lamps look like beady eyes peering down from the ceiling. All the elements make for a very interesting corner in this home.

Here, repurposed pottery ware boards have been used as a backdrop, supporting an all-wood display. Exposed lightbulbs add to the simplicity of the vision, while vintage brushes, string, beads, and a rolled-up map are a rare treat for the eye.

RIGHT An upturned wooden crate provides the surface for this open cupboard/shelf. Although apparently random, the objects on top of the shelf have actually been organized with a degree of care and thought. This collection of harmonious vintage finds are all pulled together by the vintage sign behind.

BELOW Simple shelves against glossy white paneling show off the dark wooden box on wheels and old printers' blocks, used to spell out the name of a special person or place.

A shelf for me doesn't have to hang from a wall. Any flat horizontal surface will do for displaying any items I might choose, decorative or functional. During my image research for this book, I came across many new or out-of-the-ordinary ideas for shelves, many of which I have included. Let them inspire you to move away from the conventional and discover lots of original and flexible surfaces. If you think of yourself as a curator, you may find it easier to place precious items for maximum exposure, out of harm's way, while making them look as good as you can.

A stone fire surround provides the display surface for this pair of rough vases. This is a minimal scene, but well balanced. I like the spindly twigs, which give some height, and the tiny copper lidded pot—a relief from the neutral shades.

OPPOSITE A white ball-and-claw tub looks so romantic in this rustic cabin. The collection of stone and pottery vases and pitchers is visually pleasing but, positioned on a low-level shelf, they are also within easy reach of the bather.

RIGHT Attached to this wooden beam is a metal brush clip holding a selection of awesome brushes, each with a particular purpose and uniformly placed for both ease and visual effect.

ABOVE Upside-down aged pitchers are a very pleasing shape for a decorative display. The short one in the middle provides the balance.

RIGHT This display has a strong typographic theme, with various artifacts pulled together to achieve a wonderful composition. Hanging metal letter stencils on a length of string from a hook on the wall adds height, which makes the overall display appear more balanced.

OPPOSITE Practical and decorative, this wall-hanging shelf unit has been made out of planks of reclaimed wood. The collection of vintage kitchen items adds just the right amount of character. The items are well placed but accessible, which is always a consideration in a working kitchen.

In this shot of the same high-ceilinged room shown on page 77, a simple shelf offers an opportunity for a display of various vintage pieces made of wood, carefully placed to offer shape and form.

MATINEE SAT.

Perfectly curated, this display has all the hallmarks of a really good #shelfie: Height, layers, mixed materials, the inclusion of the wall behind, and a powerful theme.

ABOVE The white-painted wall ensures that everything shown on this traditional dresser is clearly visible. Informal and practical pewter plates, layered over wooden chargers, are ready to be grabbed when setting the table. Stacks of stone dishes and wooden bowls add to the raw nature of the display.

Our gardens, the countryside, and woodland are our friends when we start to curate raw or natural #shelfies. I'm always in the garden, collecting twigs and branches to add to my various displays. The weirder their shape, the better, with random or curved offering a welcome break from square edges and solid surfaces. Placed in glass among metal or wood, these natural elements are so simple yet altogether pleasing.

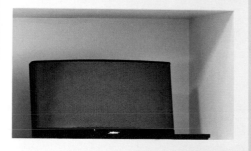

CHAPTER 4

#shelfwall

Oxford **ARCHITECTURE**
MODERN SLANG
IDIOMS
CAMBRIDGE
SYNONYMS & ANTONYMS

A well-designed shelfwall provides both useful storage and a canvas for trying out exciting, ever-changing displays.

Impactful
design solutions

A shelfwall, or wall of shelves, depending on your viewpoint, can either divide a room or become a part of the room's furniture. If you decide to use shelves to divide a big space, they need to be deep and wide. They shouldn't be completely filled, otherwise they will feel looming, and it's particularly important for a display of such a size to be well curated. Leave plenty of space to see through to the other side of the room or include some kind of opening. Beware of the danger of filling up bookshelves with books or files for the sake of it—this makes the shelves time-consuming to clean and it is also more difficult to access their contents.

PAGE 90 This illustrates the perfect shelfwall, built especially for this room. It is a practical solution for storing and displaying books, art, and other treasures. With such a large wall, it's particularly important to avoid any clutter and to keep on top of editing the contents.

PAGE 91 Clear desk, clear head is what springs to mind when looking at this home office. It is a joy to behold, with its beautiful custom-made shelfwall, neatly stacked with box files, separated by color, on one side and reference books on the other.

LEFT The rich red paintwork of the shelf recesses adds a luxuriant note to this beautiful formal space, as well as giving the books a more distinguished feel. Including a shelf above the door makes the most of the available space.

OPPOSITE These shelves are filled to the brim with books that have been color-coded. Achieving this must have been a labor of love, but the effect is stunning.

A lot of books will create a library effect in your own home, which I like, although it does require great discipline to keep them in order, otherwise the display will end up looking like a secondhand bookstore. Arranging the titles according to the color of their spines is one way to inject some order, although finding a particular book quickly won't be easy. Mixing up the way you show the books, with some stacked and others upright, injects a little variety and makes a display more attractive.

OPPOSITE Custom-made to fit a restricted space, this slanted bookshelf is a real talking point, with pleasing splashes of color from the book spines. Alongside sits a reclaimed wooden shelf unit with a delightful collection of colorful toys and models.

ABOVE Recessed shelves designed as part of the wall make an impactful entrance to the adjacent room. The objects on display are very well curated and neatly spaced on the shelves, creating uniformity and order, which is very pleasing to the eye.

RIGHT Ingenious joinery is at work here. The curve of the bottom shelf, with its caravan of dice, follows the rise of the stairs. CDs sit snugly on the higher shelves.

LEFT An extraordinary and really beautiful, custom-made unit in the home of a clever and creative individual plays host to hero objects of all shapes and sizes. These trend-driven decorative items are really allowed to sing in this space, framed by the black-painted, step-effect window.

BELOW LEFT A cleverly positioned filter of light from the ceiling window casts light over the dark shelves. This office space has clearly been designed for both a design esthetic and practicality.

RIGHT Smart and high spec, this shelf system suits the professional feel of the office and the senior role of its occupant. Keeping the shelves quite sparse gives the desired sense of gravitas to the room.

The statement walls shown here, which create the right feel for a senior executive's or professional's office, are in stark contrast to those shown in the previous chapter. These are more considered and to a higher specification.

There are so many different types of shelfwalls to choose from, either off-the-shelf or customized. If your needs are very specific, a good joiner or carpenter is always an asset and working with them to hone your ideas is vital.

At the design stage, take into account how you will use the shelves—whether they're purely for decoration, to create a certain image, or simply practical and hardworking. And don't overlook the amount of stuff you have to put on them.

OPPOSITE What a magnificent dividing shelfwall, with shelves for display and cupboards for hiding, looking through into the adjacent room. The angled wall decorated with banana palm leaf wallpaper adds to the really dramatic decorative statement.

LEFT Extreme order and color coordination are the main features of this shelf unit, with the contents as neat as a pin and mostly color-blocked for effect. I feel as if the owner is really fastidious about their belongings and knows where everything is, which, in my view, isn't such a bad thing.

Sometimes things don't have to be explained—just seeing an amazing image can set off something in your mind without the need for words.

The principles behind #shelfie displays don't really apply to shelfwalls because they have a different role. Most shelfwalls have a roof and recessed shelves, and are about organization and order, or just straightforward display. However, we still need inspiration and guidance, to help us achieve the best possible displays with them. Going through hundreds of images for this book and grouping them into categories made me realize how we live with more of our belongings on show than ever before, which makes us much more aware of what we have. I think that's a good thing.

OPPOSITE In an extremely well-thought-out and imaginative design, every inch of the wall has been used to create an impressive shelf unit. Following the line of the roof, recessed shelves of different shapes and sizes hold a wealth of personal treasures. Stairs to a mezzanine level blend seamlessly into the shelves, a very well thought out design.

Large open-plan kitchens are about having everything on show. Effectively marking the transition from the kitchen space to the living area, this boldly painted shelf unit is filled with an eclectic mix of decorative items, from Coca-Cola bottles and practical books to a mask and a pair of antlers.

LEFT More and more people now work from home and need shelf units to do a practical job. However, it's important that they blend in with the decor and don't appear too office-like. Modern, clean, and white, these shelves in an orderly light-filled home office fit the bill perfectly. Who wouldn't want to work in such an environment?

BELOW LEFT A piece of vintage furniture has been artfully transformed into a wall unit, which serves a very practical purpose, displaying groups of pretty china and glassware. But it is also very decorative and makes a strong personal statement. The importance of having a theme is very much in evidence.

RIGHT These tall bookcases make a striking statement with their confident use of color. I like how the pink fabric breaks up the wall, and how the colored glass pitcher and vase coordinate with the small chests running along the top. Incorporating other objects in among the books softens the whole effect.

OPPOSITE A real sense of unity prevails in this space that looks onto the kitchen—in fact, the entire home speaks with the same voice. These beautiful shelves have such a sense of style and are carefully curated, with small tasteful decorative items as well as books carefully placed, with their colors linking.

ABOVE LEFT There is a strong, almost museum-like theme and style to this dividing unit. Each cubbyhole contains a single item that is just the right size for the space—any more and they would appear overcrowded—which keeps everything light and airy.

ABOVE RIGHT A proper solid, floor-to-ceiling bookcase, complete with a ladder to reach the top shelves. The vivid red and pink of the folders, which I love, provide the theme. Think how different the bookcase would look simply by changing the colors of the items on it.

PAGES 106–107 What a bold, stunning statement this shelf unit makes. It adds a strong mid-century vibe to the space, in keeping with the other furniture in the room. The central wood panels cleverly conceal a television—it's sometimes nice not to have a TV on show. The room suffers no ill effect from such an imposing piece. In fact, it adds a real sense of style.

Open shelves allow extra light into the windowless space beyond and allow more of the picture wall, which acts like a backdrop in the distance, to be seen from the sleeping area. A few choice objects on the shelves, such as the brightly colored flowers, add warmth and personality to the display.

PAGE 109 Symmetrical and uncluttered, this is an impressive wall unit, comprising a mix of storage and display. The strong colors in the artwork and little pops of color from some of the objects break up the expanse of white, to make the piece even more appealing. The slanted bookshelf, glimpsed to the left of the photograph, is seen in more detail on page 94.

OPPOSITE Unevenly spaced shelves are a perfect fit for their contents, giving a pleasing discipline to the wall. The top of the low-level cabinet beneath acts as an additional shelf.

ABOVE Bookshelves take up almost an entire outside wall, even framing the window to the garden beyond. Decorative objects are scattered here and there for additional interest, while speakers are nestled in among books to help disguise them.

We have seen lots of bookshelves in this chapter and the lesson we should learn is that discipline is needed to make them look good and remain so. Books say a lot about who we are, so take care of them. Regular editing of the books displayed is essential. Coordinate them according to size and color, and never pile junk on the shelves just because there is space.

Try breaking up rows of books with some that are stacked on their sides, to change the pace. Add variety with a vase of colored glass that matches some of the books, or a plant, especially one that tumbles down, which is a good foil for books. Break up a line of books with something in a bold color, such as a large box file.

Collections of books or magazines make particularly rewarding displays. I asked my brother to build me some shelves solely for my *Vogue* magazines. Being able to pluck an issue from the shelf to see how fashion and interiors have changed over time is both exciting and refreshing. My magazines are precious, as I'm sure are all the books seen in this chapter. There are so many inspirational book display ideas here for neat freaks as well as more carefree collectors. Every collection is unique, and yours will be too.

RIGHT This really is the most dramatic bookshelf, with a stunning show of books. Notice the color blocking here and there, the various objects breaking up the display, the stacked magazines, and eccentric additions, such as the doll.

#pureandsimple

A plain white fire surround hosts a very simple and evenly spaced curation of kitchen implements. The overlapping white ceramic pieces provide depth, the wooden board and spoon height, and the single-stem dried grass texture. The framed pictures encapsulate the kitchen/dining theme.

Embrace the power of neutral colors and a few well-chosen items that speak volumes.

Less is more for a beautiful display

Your style of #shelfie says a lot about you. Those in this chapter are all gentle and inspiring. They show that a few but well-chosen items that sit well in their environment can pack a powerful punch. Restricting the color palette, often using just white, heeds the less-is-more approach, and makes an elegant statement. Sometimes it is the design of a piece that sets the tone, from a simple thrown pot or a carved wooden spoon to classic objects that have stood the test of time, and this style of display is the perfect method to show a treasured piece to make sure it stands out.

PAGE 117 I love the stark monochrome look of this kitchen display, with everything above the black cupboards and sink white or plain glass. The two long shelves are filled with beautiful all-white china: a stunning vintage pitcher collection along the top, and plates set upright on the shelf below.

ABOVE LEFT This #shelfie is an almost gallery-like solution for displaying a collection of unique pieces in a small space, with a long plank of wood holding small square uniform shelves.

ABOVE RIGHT The white metal filing cabinet gives an industrial feel to a special collection of ceramics and glass, with two turquoise pieces adding a pop of color.

Sometimes the simple things are the hardest to display, and you can spend a long time placing objects until you have the balance just right or making sure that a hint of color doesn't look out of place.

A sense of order is generally called for. Give your objects a formal structure, perhaps putting them in a row, and then make small adjustments. The #shelfie rules still apply to pure and simple displays with fewer items—tall at the back, the largest off-center, layering for depth, using the wall behind as a backdrop. A simple display is possible with any color, but all-white on all-white is wonderful, as is all-black on all-black.

The orderliness of the shelves in this functional and stylish kitchen makes them easy to navigate, use, and maintain. Stacks of plates and neat rows of china and glassware, arranged according to size and function, are close to hand as well as pleasing to the eye.

OPPOSITE This cottage epitomizes a pure and simple decorative style. Making straightforward choices—white walls, white shelves, the palest gray linen, and some pale gray glass—is a very good place to start on a homemaking journey. This is a calm and tranquil scene, uncluttered and unfussy, with a well-curated display.

ABOVE Three ceramic vessels in different shades of turquoise, and a blue crackled yogurt pot holding an incense stick, marry well with the stoneware and rough concrete shelf.

RIGHT One vase, one candle, and one artwork on the mantel of a white-painted Victorian fireplace is as simple as a #shelfie gets. Just perfect.

Vintage markets and antique shops are the places to go for collectibles, but if you're more interested in contemporary pottery or supporting local artists, try visiting art fairs. I've embraced many decorating styles over the years because my career in home buying exposed me to the ever-changing world of trends, color palettes, and designers. Some of my most precious items will always be on display, while others are banished to the closet. My favorite things take on a whole new look when there is space around them or they are allowed to sit alone. I love how a pure and simple style can help achieve these transformations, and in the process help you to become more creative.

TOP LEFT A single-stem flower in a glass container is the most creative way of displaying flowers when keeping to a simple style. The pop of pink from these blooms adds vibrancy to the muted mantel display.

LEFT Vintage ceramic and enamel pieces from a collection themed around drinking and dining sit well together on the shelves of this old white dresser. Each piece is allowed to tell its own story in this uncluttered display.

OPPOSITE Tiny floating shelves, with room enough only for a single artisan teacup on each, make an impactful and inspiring display lined up alongside an old ladder. The regular spacing throughout creates a delightful symmetry.

Old wooden crates, turned on their sides and painted white, are a practical and attractive way to display everyday kitchen implements. Separating out the various pieces according to how they are used brings discipline to the display.

ABOVE With a paneled wall as a backdrop, a plain white shelf houses two ammonites and a smaller group of fossils and stones. Collected from the beach, they make the perfect #shelfie in this seaside cottage. Off-center height for added interest is provided by the framed dried leaves.

ABOVE RIGHT Two opposing items in every way—an old carved Indian ox and a thoroughly modern piece of fine pottery—make an unlikely pairing but one that pays off.

I like to see a shelf with just a few simple but unusual items displayed on it, reaffirming my #shelfie rules and disciplines. There is a common thread running through the images on these pages, and all of them, whether they appeal to you or not, adhere to these rules. The displays feature several strong looks. They mix old with new, keep to a rigid color theme with just a pop of color, create a natural display with a real sense of balance, a story, and a solid color backdrop.

Modern arrangements in a traditional house are the epitome of today's stylish interiors, and owners use many clever ideas to update and upgrade their period homes. But it can be just as rewarding to make such displays

in keeping with the traditional style of the building. My feeling is that the look you establish is a matter of personal taste. After all, your home is where you want to feel the most relaxed and happy, and surrounding yourself with the important things in your life is what matters. Irrespective of your chosen style, keep a clear vision and a clear mind. Stick to your original idea and don't let clutter get in the way.

ABOVE LEFT A white-painted vintage shelf unit with hooks underneath and a selection of vintage enamel and ceramic pieces make the perfect pure display in a whitewashed seaside cottage. All the items share the same voice and sit so well together. I love how the pop of red brings the display to life.

ABOVE The dark painted walls reflected in this mirror give the illusion of an empty frame—I was fooled until I realized that the light fitting was reflected in it. It's a simple but very effective idea, and only a few small items are needed to complete this #shelfie.

PAGES 128 & 129 Two perfect still-life images, beautifully and artfully created. The detailing of the dark objects against the dark walls and shelves is quite exquisite, while the luster of the metallic tones gives a feeling of opulence. Even the dark leaf has been chosen to support the very intense and bold statement. Although there is a lot of black in these #shelfies, the interest comes from the different textures.

Particular design periods, such as modernist or mid-century, often have particular colors, textiles, materials, and shapes associated with them. Using them in your #shelfies to evoke a certain era can have a powerful effect on the whole display image.

In a strong period #shelfie, the pop of orange glass brings the 1950s and '60s vividly to life. Even the textured wallpaper harks back to the era. The varied heights of the different objects give the display added interest, as does the mix of textured and smooth surfaces. Two simple seeded stalks introduce just the right amount of foliage.

Monochrome is a very powerful decorating palette and one that's easy to use, whether with dark walls and white shelves or the other way around. A reduced palette makes choosing and displaying objects much simpler, provided that the principles of display (see page 6) are followed. Shape and form play an integral part, and experimenting with different textures is the way to introduce subtle differences to the overall display.

I've used a lot of black and white in my apartment, and now I'm starting to add brown and raw wood. A tiny bit of wood in the middle of a predominantly monochrome #shelfie in a kitchen is subtle and pleasing—think of the stark white of everyday white china punctuated with a carved wooden bowl or a tall vase of twigs.

ABOVE The contrasting shapes of the tall, thin vase in pale gray and the fatter black vase are perfectly placed off-center on a white recessed shelf, alongside the black-and-white photo, which makes the display personal. The top shelf is equally well balanced.

LEFT This calm, pared-back space tells a very simple monochrome story. I love the scale of the pendant light against the objects on display. The tall, black vase makes a lovely pairing with the small, white pot.

OPPOSITE There is a great deal of drama in this kitchen, with its jet black walls, cabinets, and shelves making a striking modern statement. The look is dense and very pure, not to mention inspiring. The white china appears to be floating on the black shelves, while the glasses dangle cleverly from the bottom shelf. Relief from the black in this very disciplined space is provided by the wooden worktop and stools.

OPPOSITE These recessed kitchen shelves above a marble worktop are designed for the specific purpose of efficiency and accessibility to items used every day. They are also visually pleasing. Beneath the worktop, double-recessed shelves provide even more storage space.

ABOVE LEFT In this simple but decorative white-on-white display, a molded fire surround is highlighted by the beautiful Pols Potten ceramic vase and flower relief tile.

ABOVE CENTER The reflection in the mirror of the wall opposite makes the mirror appear the same shade. The overlapping mug has been deliberately chosen for its color match.

ABOVE RIGHT It is worth having shelves made to suit particular needs. Small but deep, this well-crafted wooden shelf has been specially designed to house a selection of teapots.

If you can have your shelves made, I always advise that you select your own materials and brackets. The shelves should be made exactly to fit, look perfect in the space chosen for them, and be strong enough to hold the weight required of them. I had my kitchen shelves made by my builder when the kitchen was being installed, and I have never looked back. They fit perfectly over the kitchen sink unit, and it's easy to grab hold of my everyday mugs, plates, and so on. I enjoy keeping the top shelf as a creative display-shelf. It has had many guises over the years in keeping with the latest trends. I have bought shelves from chain stores in the past, but have ended up being disappointed because they are not sturdy and fit for purpose.

A beautiful, slim console by Uhuru Design allows each piece arranged on it to be a hero in its own right. A traditionally shaped Wedgwood vase, a plate, and a bowl are carefully placed for a sense of harmony. All the objects are simple, monochromatic, and with rustic textures—the large, white dried leaf adds a quirky twist. It is a shelf display that speaks volumes about the care that has been taken when arranging this collection.

RIGHT A black wall and black shelves are the perfect combination to show off everyday china and glassware. This is a thoughtful and balanced presentation, with the stacked bowls, a single teapot, utilitarian glasses, and the angle of the teacups creating a pleasing effect, and all are slightly off-center.

BELOW A single shelf with simple Japanese ceramic bowls in an undulating row, with added height and color provided by the black bottle, and depth by the round vase. The arrangement allows for the appreciation of these handmade craft ceramics—each piece is different but, displayed as a collection, the unique shapes and colors offset all the others.

This imaginative shelving space echoes the shape of the bedroom under the eaves. Not only is it visually stunning, but it's also just the right size to hold bedtime reads.

The thick recessed shelves
built into this beautiful
bathroom are painted the
same shade as the walls. This
allows the white objects, both
decorative and functional, to
punctuate the space. Items
purely for decoration are
reserved for the top shelf,
while those with a practical
use are on the lower shelves
for easy access.

#recycled

With a little bit of imagination and skill, a truly unique style will emerge from combining vintage finds.

Surprising ideas
from the unusual

It is always a thrill to find an ingenious new use for something old and give it a chance at another life. Flea markets and antiques fairs are great places to discover old wood and architectural salvage to use as shelving. Weathered floorboards, old school furniture, carts from bakeries, or simply wood from historic buildings that have been demolished are finds that always have character, from their mysterious layers of paint to beautiful detailing. Whether incorporated into a new structure or reused in their current form to make shelves, the creative ideas on the following pages will hopefully spark your imagination so you can create displays that are truly unique.

PAGE 142 What a find! This vintage industrial cart, probably used on a factory floor at the turn of the 20th century, is now a really practical and useful shelf unit. The wheels add to its versatility.

PAGE 143 Tall salvaged wooden structures have been cleverly and imaginatively turned into vertical bookshelves, secured to the wall.

OPPOSITE Hung tightly together, some very worn metal cabinets, which were probably once used as bathroom or medicine cabinets, have been stripped back to their raw state. One has had its doors removed to become an open shelf display. It now provides a fitting backdrop for some beautiful Dylan Bowen ceramics.

RIGHT This library stepladder has been put to good domestic use, its tall handles creating a perfect side table bookshelf, with enough space to display a vase of decorative flowers.

BELOW This is a masterclass in recycling. An old wooden pallet fixed to the wall makes the perfect rack for a display of artisan plates, while pieces of reclaimed wood have been made into doors for the concrete kitchen units. The vibrant colors of the pieces on display harmonize beautifully with the salvaged wood, creating a beautiful kitchen with so much character.

My advice is always to keep an eye out for carts and ladders because they can be reused to create some interesting shelving. Sometimes it's such unexpected items that make the most useful additions to the home. Old floorboards and planks of wood from, say, bakeries or shoe factories, can be turned into original shelf units. Any carpenter will make them fit for purpose. Make sure that you check for woodworm. If the infestation isn't active or widespread, you can treat it quite easily and ensure that it won't spread to other items in your home. I like to leave layers of paint or varnish on anything I salvage because they add so much character to a piece.

LEFT A fascinating curation of interesting objects, all from former factories that made either shoes or hats. The two carts, which may have been used in a shoe factory, have been strengthened by the addition of new shelves.

OPPOSITE Against the mole-colored wall paint, the salvaged shelves fit perfectly in this room. Holding a collection of books, artworks, and objects, reinforced metal struts make this a completely solid unit, which sits well on the rustic floorboards.

OPPOSITE & LEFT A large, light-filled loft has been converted into a really cool apartment and work space, which retains the original metal-framed windows, poured concrete floors, and industrial radiators. The shelves—planks of wood balanced between ladders—also make perfect room dividers and suit the surroundings very well.

BELOW Wire-mesh shelves, which look as though they were originally used for organizing letters in a sorting office, make the ideal ready-made shelving unit—solid and practical—standing on this desk.

Paint-spattered ladders are a joy to find. They tell the story of busy decorators who have used them over the years, and the markings and patterns simply can't be recreated. Making unique room dividers with long planks of wood balanced between ladders is easy to do—no sawing or screwing required. They can be moved easily and can be extended when needed, as well as being really sturdy, making them perfect for bookshelves.

Some of my favorite places to spark the imagination are salvage and reclamation yards, which deal in home clearance and the demolition of old buildings and factories. The treasures to be found there are endless, and with everything at much more reasonable prices than at flea markets, they really are the unsung heroes of the interior design world.

OPPOSITE TOP LEFT This display has taken some imagination and a good dose of humor to create. An old medicine chest has been given a new lease of life as a shoe cabinet in the entrance hall and become an immediate talking point for first-time visitors.

OPPOSITE TOP RIGHT Most likely from a disused factory, this magnificent cabinet adds character to the room and is a very useful piece of furniture.

OPPOSITE BOTTOM LEFT Stacked apple crates turned on their side add character to a room and offer lots of open storage and display space.

OPPOSITE BOTTOM RIGHT Pieces like this vintage post office sorting unit give an industrial touch to a home. It has been reinvented here as pantry storage in a kitchen.

ABOVE A jigsaw of vintage fruit crates creates a really interesting composition. Choose a mix of sizes to accommodate your objects, as in this thoughtfully chosen selection of crates that holds the owner's prized collection of Brown Betty teapots and pitchers.

I love finding items that have an array of different uses. My favorites are crates of all kinds, but particularly fruit crates, many of which come with markings and stickers that illustrate how they were used originally. Crates can be painted, but they can also be used in their raw state. Whether hung or stacked, they make perfect storage or display units, their varying shapes offering relief from uniformity and allowing you to place objects of different sizes within them. I frequently use crates for everyday storage needs. Being so portable and adaptable, they can act as anything from bedside tables to kitchen shelving. Another idea is to paint a few in bright citrus colors to be used as fun and useful bookshelves in a child's bedroom. You can keep adding crates as the book collection expands.

Two magnificent units from a salvage company, seen here and opposite, have almost become part of the wall. With its narrow shelves, it is totally perfect for showing a selection of postcards—or any other treasures that may require a more delicate approach to their display.

An eclectic and unusual array of vintage cupboards, crates, and cabinets provide the necessary storage and display space for a busy crafter. Decorative open crates are just the right shape and size to house small sewing accessories as well as personal treasures.

ABOVE It's likely that this large reclaimed china display unit, still being used as it was originally intended, came from a factory in the UK, where there was once a thriving ceramics industry. Sadly, this has diminished over the years and, as a result, such items are reasonably easy to find at antiques markets and salvage yards.

ABOVE RIGHT A large, metal-framed baker's rack is put to great use as a storage unit for shoes, keeping them neat and tidy. The wheels make the piece flexible, but the best thing is that you can see all your shoes at a glance.

The vintage style seen here will go perfectly in a period house, but adding pieces of salvage to an ultra-modern home can also look wonderful. Although modern design brings efficiency and clean lines, any character it lacks can be introduced with the ideas illustrated on these pages. Mid-century furniture, raw wood, and beautifully aged walls can all create something unique and full of character for your displays. Next time you are at a flea market and notice some lovely weathered storage units, think about how you can integrate them into your own home.

Three crates hung side by side above a desk create just the right amount of shelf space for reference books and papers in this cool office. The giant pencil adds a quirky touch, while the yellow metal industrial cart, possibly from a factory, makes a useful mobile storage unit for other office accessories.

#shelvesofcuriosities

Lime-plastered walls and a high ledge above a plain fireplace is the perfect platform for antique curios. The antlers—set off-center—add shape, texture, and height. Almost all the objects come as a pair, creating perfect harmony and order in a well-balanced shelf display that adds interest to an elegant room.

OPPOSITE A dark-wood cabinet makes the perfect home for a cornucopia of curios—coral, shells, a pretty landscape painting, mercury vases of varying heights, a vintage shell-covered jewelry box—that has the natural world at its heart.

Well-chosen objects create a sense of wonder,
and natural colors and textures are celebrated.

More is more

This chapter, which is dear to my heart, is all about maximalism—more is more, I say! I've always been an avid flea market shopper and collector. Displaying my finest treasures is important to me, and I often rotate my pieces because I have so many of them. Cabinets of curiosities first appeared in 16th-century Europe. Also known as "wonder rooms," they were small collections of extraordinary objects from natural history, geology, ethnography, and archeology, and religious or historical relics, works of art, and antiquities. You can use the same principles to create your own cabinet, keeping in mind the core of maximalism and magic. The fun is in the creation—I often take everything off my shelves and start all over again because you never know

what you might end up with. It's worth remembering that for a busy display to be effective and stay looking its best, it has to be dust-free and clean.

Grouping the same objects in different patterns is a great idea, or you could go for a more ordered look by putting similar colors and materials together, and a story will emerge. One of my favorite things about cabinets of curiosities is that they are such talking points. With so many interesting objects on display, they invite scrutiny, and the objects almost ask to be handled. That is all to the good, because it will encourage you to play around with the display. This is all about having fun, using your imagination, and delighting in the unexpected.

ABOVE A wooden shelf fixed to a raw brick wall is laden with an eclectic and colorful mix of ornaments, including a fish-shaped pitcher, Greek amphoras, miniature goblets, and a rather solid-looking statue. Although the pieces almost touch the ceiling and look a little crowded, this shelf display is above all else very balanced and orderly.

OPPOSITE Grouping a collection on a narrow table against a wall makes a lovely backdrop for a sofa—as long as it is far enough away so that you don't hit your head—together with the hanging art. The height levels in this display are perfect, from the pictures on the wall to the smaller leaning photos and the off-center group of glass. I like the pops of turquoise and blue in the glass and art, which pull the vision together.

OPPOSITE This bathroom dresser houses an original complementary grouping. Cubes and bars of soap are jumbled together behind the glass doors, along with some vintage boxes of laundry detergent. The top of the dresser has been used as a shelf for a portrait and three vintage enamel pitchers. Although this is an eclectic mix, it is not at all out of place in a bathroom.

ABOVE A shelf or table by a window benefits from changing light throughout the day. Here, a shaft of light creates a lovely still-life, borrowing ideas from Dutch 17th-century painters. Some treasured items, displayed with plenty of space between them, create a very tranquil image.

RIGHT A subtle theme established around a common color, with a complementary pop of pink, offset by gray shelves on matching gray walls.

Although I have tried to show shelves from different types of homes and in different styles, all the displays have one thing in common: they are made up of personal treasures belonging to a family or an individual, beautiful things that have been collected over the years, perhaps brought home by children or given by a loved one. When I write about #shelfie rules, sometimes they simply do not apply. Whether a home is stuffed with eclectic paintings, glass and ceramics, or jewelry, one thing is for sure—if you think something has a place on your shelves, it does.

Although this collection is made up of a seemingly disparate mix of objects, it has obviously been put together by one person. It has a feminine feel, with rose string lights entwined around the pieces on the shelf, wa beautifully ornate mirror placed off-center, and an antique bust wearing a hat set at a jaunty angle.

OPPOSITE TOP LEFT An old stone ledge and a large piece of slate used as a backdrop give this #shelfie a natural frame, the rough surfaces complementing those of the pots and vases.

OPPOSITE TOP RIGHT The recessed shelf of a tall, white wall unit makes an ideal display space for some treasured ceramics.

OPPOSITE BOTTOM LEFT Two white floating shelves—almost invisible against the white wall— greet visitors to this home. Treasured items are displayed on them in a weekly rotation, so that I never know what I'm going to see the next time I visit.

OPPOSITE BOTTOM RIGHT Acting as a backdrop, a sheet of zinc or a blackboard, as shown here, gives focus and depth to a shelf display. A painted board or an empty picture frame—with the colors changed every so often for variety—could also be used.

ABOVE A beautiful, mostly monochrome vignette is offset by the pale delicate flowers and foliage, which bring softness.

These days I do like to use black in decoration, as well as for my clothes, and the opportunities to add a pop of color are frequent. Black picture frames and vases are paired with color hinted at in paintings or plants and flowers, all a reminder that objects from nature make the best accessories, their soft forms breaking up hard lines and adding height. The changing seasons often bring fresh ideas and mean that a display can be ever- evolving as spring blossom branches are replaced with fragrant flowers and fall leaves.

PAGES 170–171 This ultimate cabinet of curiosities conveys a powerful sense of nature. Shells, coral, and antlers share the matt black shelves with a central piece of black-and-white photographic art, introduced for balance. This is a well-curated and utterly dynamic display.

The shelves depicted on these pages aren't for everyone—they have a distinct style that would leave minimalists cold. My advice for creating such maximalist displays would be to start small and build your collection slowly by shelf and by type, otherwise you run the risk of creating chaos and being accused of hoarding.

A well-balanced maximalist display has its place even in a relatively simple space, but try to keep it at just the one. It's easy to end up with too much—and I am definitely one of those people, because I find it so hard to pass up something beautiful—so always be discerning. Ask yourself whether something will add a missing element to your display, and whether it has a home within the theme you have chosen.

PAGES 172 & 173 These dark rooms with their dark shelves, enhanced with contrasting objects and books, look almost magical. On the right, a large, fan-shaped piece of fake coral and sparkling string lights add to the ethereal nature of the display. The overall effect in both rooms is pure drama.

BELOW Two sturdy shelves house a pleasingly coherent collection of china. Decorative pieces are displayed on the top shelf, with the largest element placed off-center, and all the everyday items on the bottom. With such open and accessible shelving, it is quick and easy to replace objects or swap them around for a change of scene.

OPPOSITE A large antique medicine cabinet in its original state has been filled to the brim with all sorts of interesting objects. Most of them are made of glass or metal, which gives order to the display.

OPPOSITE A glass-fronted cabinet holds everything that is precious to its owner, from travel souvenirs and photographs of loved ones to pretty pebbles picked up from the beach during memorable vacations. The bright white paneled shelves and background give a fresh and modern feel without a hint of stuffiness.

ABOVE Despite being completely eccentric, this display in an old apple crate is very well considered. It has been put together with thought and skill, so that all the items complement one another.

RIGHT A really tiny shelf made out of a little wooden crate holds a dollhouse-style display. The colors of the minuscule desk and chair are picked out in the glass jars of pigment arranged on top.

PAGES 178–179 This is a masterclass in the curation of some rather dark objects. Setting the tone for the strong, distinct style is the austere art piece over the mantel, which is home to some very interesting and well-chosen pieces. These are evenly spaced out, with the tallest items—a stack of books and a lamp—positioned off-center.

OPPOSITE Although this cabinet is in a home, it has been curated with such care and precision that it could be in a museum. The artfully placed skulls, shells, and architectural fragments mean each vignette in the display has its own merit.

ABOVE Imperfection sums up this collector's objective in their search for all things old and interesting. Grouped together, they tell a story. I also like vintage objects arranged along stark shelves. Height is provided by the barometer, the nostalgic paper package creates depth and texture, and the broken glass bowl gives everything an offbeat twist. The toys and candy beads add humor.

My adage when arranging large groups of objects is to create vignettes, with each one telling its own story. This is one of my main principles (see page 6), and creating scenes allows you to achieve a sense of clarity in an otherwise exuberant display.

A common thread running through these shelves is nature. It provides so many materials for displays, which can be changed along with the seasons. Collecting on country walks and vacations provides a unique reference and is a reminder of a place in time.

Old books are essential for supporting displays—simply stack them and arrange an object on top. Choose them for the color of their cover or binding, or even place them with the spine facing inward on the shelf so they become a display feature.

The quirkiness and sense of fun present in this #shelfie reveal the personality of the owner. Above the off-center clock, the painting, which is positioned centrally over the shelf, shows a woman gazing down ironically at the viewer. As you can see, not many of my display rules have been followed here, but nevertheless this is a #shelfie that works very well.

ABOVE This display at a vintage market stall hits all the right notes. An old cake tin provides a platform for the small Japanese doll, a mannequin head with an askew hat is positioned off-center, and an ostrich feather and fake roses provide vibrant color and texture. It is an ordered jumble, just what you want when rummaging for vintage clothes and accessories.

I've talked a lot about my rules for displays, but don't forget that they are meant to be broken. The core ideas are perfect while you are finding your feet, but in the end if you trust your instincts, they will lead you to do what is right for your home and your collections. Only you know what sort of home you have, how you live there, and what look you are going for. This book has given you plenty of food for thought—it's good to know some basics so you know what to rebel against—so just keep experimenting. Remember that a shelf display is at its most striking when it's yours and yours alone and shows off your unique personality and the things that you love.

OPPOSITE This display is home to a
mix of useful and decorative objects.
Vintage and well-used kitchen
implements are beautiful to look
at, a stark contrast to the more
surprising elements—an animal
skull, a sculptural cauliflower inside
a bell jar, and a wooden parrot,
just for the hell of it. Above it all,
a perfectly placed antler display,
well proportioned and balanced.

ABOVE The witty collection on this
ledge, behind a looming ladder, plays
with proportion as it tells the story of
the owner, a seamstress, all the while
keeping to a neutral color palette.

RIGHT The painting on the wall
provides the off-center element in
this #shelfie, while the narrow white
vase on the bamboo shelf unit adds
height. Predominantly neutral shades
are used, with the color pink picked
out here and there for added interest.
Fans of coral provide the backdrop.

Resources

Abigail Ahern
www.abigailahern.com

Anthropologie
www.anthropologie.com

Architronic
www.architonic.com

**Ardingly International
Antiques & Collectors Fair**
South of England Showground
Ardingly

West Sussex
RH17 6TL
www.iacf.co.uk/ardingly

Baileys Home
www.baileyshome.com

Brooklyn Flea
Held at three New York locations:
Brooklyn, Fort Greene, Williamsburg
www.brooklynflea.com

Conran Shop
www.conranshop.co.uk

IKEA
www.ikea.com

Lassco
www.lassco.co.uk

Round Top Antiques Fair
Round Top
Texas
www.roundtoptexasantiques.com

String Furniture
stringfurniture.com

Sunbury Antiques Market
Kempton Park Racecourse
Staines Road East
Sunbury On Thames
TW16 5AQ
www.sunburyantiques.com/Kempton

Target
www.target.com

3Pamono
www.pamono.co.uk/shelves-wall-units

Vitsoe
www.vitsoe.com

Photography credits

All photos copyright CICO Books and Ryland Peters and Small, unless otherwise stated.

Front cover: James Gardiner; **back cover (top right):** Simon Brown; **back cover (bottom left):** Anna Williams; **back cover (bottom right):** Rachel Whiting; **endpapers:** Rachel Whiting; **page 1:** James Gardiner; **page 2:** Rachel Whiting; **page 3:** Debi Treloar; **page 4:** Rachel Whiting; **pages 7-8:** Rachel Whiting; **page 10:** Rachel Whiting; **page 11:** Catherine Gratwicke; **page 12:** Debi Treloar; **page 13:** Catherine Gratwicke; **page 14:** Andrew Wood; **page 15 (top):** Paul Massey; **page 15 (bottom):** Emma Mitchell; **pages 16-17:** Jan Baldwin; **page 18 (top left):** Rachel Whiting; **page 18 (top right):** James Gardiner; **page 18 (bottom left):** Rachel Whiting; **page 18 (bottom right):** Rachel Whiting; **page 19-20:** Catherine Gratwicke; **pages 22-23:** Emma Mitchell; **page 24:** Catherine Gratwicke; **page 25 (left):** Jan Baldwin; **page 25 (right):** Catherine Gratwicke; **page 26:** Catherine Gratwicke; **page 27:** Andrew Wood; **page 29:** Debi Treloar; **page 30-32:** Rachel Whiting; **page 33:** Emma Mitchell; **page 34:** Jan Baldwin; **page 35 (top):** Rachel Whiting; **page 35 (bottom):** Catherine Gratwicke; **page 36:** Andrew Wood; **page 38:** Earl Carter; **page 39:** Polly Wreford; **page 40:** Pia Ulin; **page 41:** Polly Wreford; **page 42:** Pia Ulin; **page 44:** Debi Treolar; **page 45 (top):** Rachel Whiting; **page 45 (bottom):** Christopher Drake; **page 46 (left):** Rachel Whiting; **page 46 (right):** Debi Treloar; **page 47 (left):** Jan Baldwin; **page 47 (right):** Polly Wreford; **page 48:** Anna Williams; **page 50 (top):** Debi Treloar; **page 50 (bottom):** Pia Ulin; **page 51:** Anna Williams; **page 52:** Jan Baldwin; **page 53:** Pia Ulin; **page 54 (left):** Polly Wreford; **page 54 (right):** Pia Ulin; **page 55:** Polly Wreford; **page 56:** Pia Ulin; **pages 58-59:** Rachel Whiting; **pages 60-64:** Debi Treloar; **page 65 (left):** Hans Blomquist & Debi Treloar; **page 65 (right):** Polly Wreford; **pages 66-69:** Debi Treloar; **page 70:** Jan Baldwin; **page 72:** Catherine Gratwicke; **page 73:** Debi Treloar; **page 74:** Hans Blomquist & Debi Treloar; **page 75:** Rachel Whiting; **pages 76-79:** Debi Treloar; **page 80:** Hans Blomquist & Debi Treloar; **page 81:** Anna Williams; **page 82:** Debi Treloar; **page 83 (top and center):** Debi Treloar; **page 83 (bottom):** Hans Blomquist & Debi Treloar; **pages 84-85:** Debi Treloar; **page 86:** Hans Blomquist & Debi Treloar; **page 87:** Debi Treloar; **page 88:** Rachel Whiting; **page 90:** Anna Williams; **pages 91-92:** Polly Wreford; **pages 93-94:** Simon Brown; **page 95 (top):** Pia Ulin; **page 95 (bottom):** Emma Mitchell;

pages 96-97: Catherine Gratwicke; **page 97:** Christopher Drake; **page 98:** Catherine Gratwicke; **page 99:** Debi Treloar; **page 100:** Rachel Whiting; **page 101:** Debi Treloar; **page 102:** Polly Wreford; **page 103:** Debi Treloar; **page 104:** Polly Wreford; **page 105 (right):** Polly Wreford; **page 106:** Catherine Gratwicke; **pages 108-109:** Simon Brown; **page 110:** Polly Wreford; **page 111:** Paul Massey; **page 112:** Debi Treloar; **page 114:** Jan Baldwin; **page 116:** Rachel Whiting; **page 117:** Polly Wreford; **page 118:** Rachel Whiting; **page 119:** Jan Baldwin; **page 120:** Rachel Whiting; **page 121 (top):** Hans Blomquist & Debi Treloar; **page 121 (bottom):** Rachel Whiting; **page 122:** Polly Wreford; **page 123:** Debi Treloar; **page 124:** Anna Williams; **page 126 (right):** Jan Baldwin; **page 127 (left):** Polly Wreford; **page 127 (right):** Debi Treloar; **pages 128-129:** Pia Ulin; **page 130:** Rachel Whiting; **page 132 (top):** Rachel Whiting; **page 132 (bottom):** Polly Wreford; **page 133:** Debi Treloar; **page 134:** Polly Wreford; **page 135 (left):** Polly Wreford; **page 135 (center):** Polly Wreford; **page 135 (right):** Debi Treloar; **page 136:** Pia Ulin; **page 137 (top):** Rachel Whiting; **page 137 (bottom):** Debi Treloar; **page 138:** Rachel Whiting; **page 139:** Pia Ulin; **page 140:** Debi Treloar; **page 142:** Catherine Gratwicke; **pages 143-147:** Debi Treloar; **page 148:** Benjamin Edwards; **page 149 (top):** Benjamin Edwards; **page 149 (bottom):** Rachel Whiting; **page 150:** Debi Treloar; **page 151 (top right):** Andrew Wood; **page 151 (top left):** Rachel Whiting; **page 151 (bottom left):** Debi Treloar; **page 151 (bottom right):** Debi Treloar; **pages 152-153:** Debi Treloar; **page 154:** Rachel Whiting; **pages 156-157:** Debi Treloar; **page 158:** Anna Williams; **page 160:** Hans Blomquist & Debi Treloar; **page 161:** Debi Treloar; **page 162:** Jan Baldwin; **page 163:** Debi Treloar; **page 164:** Anna Williams; **page 165 (top):** Anna Williams; **page 165 (bottom):** Debi Treloar; **page 166:** Jan Baldwin; **page 168 (bottom left):** Andrew Wood; **page 168 (top left, top right, and bottom right):** Anna Williams; **page 169:** Anna Williams; **pages 170-173:** Debi Treloar; **page 174:** Andrew Wood; **page 175:** Catherine Gratwicke; **pages 176-177:** Debi Treloar; **page 178:** Pia Ulin; **page 180:** Anna Williams; **pages 181-183:** Debi Treloar; **page 184:** Jan Baldwin; **page 185:** Anna Williams; **pages 186-187:** Rachel Whiting; **page 189:** Rachel Whiting; **page 190:** Debi Treloar; **page 192:** Debi Treloar.

Index

Acknowledgments

Thank you to Cindy Richards, the publisher of CICO Books, for commissioning me to write this book. Thank you also to Anna Galkina and Penny Craig. Huge thanks to Toni Kay who did a wonderful job on the layout and design, and to Helen Ridge for making sense of my words.

Thank you to my daughter Rosie for her continued help and support and to Ian Meek for providing me with a bolthole with a sea view while I was writing.

And of course, thank you to all the authors, photographers, and homeowners who enabled me to create this book from the huge library of images that they produced.